Platinum Poetry Series

I0159039

Romantics

William Driscoll

Terracom Books

Romantics
Terracom Books Platinum Poetry Series/January 2015
First Edition

Published by Terracom Books
A Division of Terracom Media

This is a work of fiction. Names, characters, places and incidents are imaginary.
Any resemblance to persons, living or dead, events or locations is entirely coincidental.
No portion of this work may be reproduced in any form or by any means without written
permission from the publisher.

All rights reserved
Copyright ©2015 by William Driscoll

ISBN–13: 978-0-692-33529-1

Terracom Media

mediaterracom@gmail.com
ghost

CONTENTS

Juliana

"sensit, ut ipsa suis aderat Venus aurea festis,
vota quid illa velint et, amici numinis omen,
flamma ter accensa est apicemque per aera duxit." [1]
~Ovid

i

The wind blows, the warm winds blow, blow
Winds of Spring, recede raw winter's gray
What can I now of Julianna say?
Oh blow wanton winds, winds of wonder blow!
Bend black bows, ice swaying in the breeze
New shoots explode those twigs to shade the day
What can I pray of Julianna say?
Amid the infant dreaming of the trees
Sing to me and in me boldly sing
As on those Aegean islands long ago
Nine voices harmonized fair Ilium's fall [2]
And lords grew grave to hear the poet's tale

ii

Smooth olive skin once fired the passionate Greek
And one face unfurled a thousand sail salute
The lion's roar, the cries of war now mute
Dull echo down the halls of history
As Tamora at vengeful Titus' feast
Still nature gnaws her offspring winter long
Till even saints must wonder what went wrong
Will none be sent to launch this island's peace?

---

1 - "Venus was present at her own festival and realized
the import of his prayer. And as a sacred sign of the
favoring deity three times, the altar flame blazed up
and propelled its point through the air."
2 - The Muses.

But 'gard in dark night's jet black velvet vaults
A light as bright as Hyperion[3] chariot–fire
Ascends, a sign to shameless blushing earth
Announcing here another blessèd birth

iii

A reflection of an ever present form
A reminder of a never ending doom
A fairy–flower that blooms in merry June
A petite prince's prize that gloom adorns
Hill and valley, hill and dale sweep
The meadows mint bejewelèd, dance along
'Tween shafts of sunlight where her silver song
Is swimming, in the moon–curled ocean deep
Round wandering May she whiles upon her way
A foster child of wind and April rain
Through Arcadian forests freed of thous and thees
Where few now seek the crown of the bay leaf trees

iv

Yes, in wild woods our fair Julianna's born
A cherub–waif of sylvan innocence
Fair nature's dying try at recompense
To you entombed in urban filth forlorn
Sweet Amaranth bedewed that blooms eternal
Soft she strolls beside the Hippocrene[4]
'Midst piercing stars and gleams of red and green
And tow'ring Yew trees, verdant blue and vernal
And by her side a fountain angel flies
As on the wing, a glistening white–shell form
'Julianna, my child, I'll fetch you a likely lad
To bring you that which only lovers have'

---

3 - In Greek mythology, the Titan god of light.
4 - The font of the Muses.

V

'Master him yet let yourself be mastered
Conquer him with sighs of sweet release
Sow your seeds where weeds will find no peace
Wrap him in your arms of alabaster!'
And with that the shinning angel left her soaring
Towards the den of men, hazing boroughs
Smoking cities, where the mortal furrows
Deep are dug yet plugged with brambles warring
Some poet, painter, hard rock sculptor, maker
Of sweet music's meter, one she sought
There were not many, to bring to the forest there
And in that lofty grove, to love her lady there

vi

Bright Kalliope[5] searched the streets of yellow-gray
For one of wild yet personal intent
But found that mortal's wayward paths were rent
From Demeter's daughter fading day by day
No longer were their heights and depths renewed
No longer did their Eros pinnacle
No longer were their trials chronicled
But pomegranates were food for ought but few
The children reaped the ripening corn, the fools
The flowers full, the madmen danced upon
The moon, riding the merry winds of June
Croaking their sharp inharmonious tune

vii

Despairing not, she sought throughout the night
For one untouched by cynical decline
For one in touch with human-kind divine
To set this dying desert land to right

---

5 - The Muse of of epic poetry.

Then 'fore the morning sun had breached the smoke
She spied in a small and humble dwelling place
A child–man with child hands and face
Asleep with boundless freedom from his yoke
In a dreamless vision she came alone to him
Passiano self-tutored in the tomes of lore
Bidding him tread the ancient forest's floor
Where Julianna awaited the opening door

viii

'Dream sleep's dreams Kalliope calls you
Dream the dreams of now immortal bards
Reach that meadow's dense and ancient yards
See that grove aglow with towering yew!'
So Passiano arose from the ken of men
To that garden formed before the mournful fall
To flowers filling, chilling towers tall
And the mystery of that meet and magic glen
There green on a hill Julianna found him
Bidding him drink and bathe in the fountain's white
The mountain's childe, idol of a Cyprian whim
Then bid him rend his heart of human spite
And rest his soul in Selene's[6] moonlight dim

ix

The waters of that vast and timeless place
Worked wonders in the boy-man's eyes of blue
He saw for miles beyond the towering yew
And gazed through heaven's gate and darkling space
'Who are you maid of beauty frightening fair?
Who takes a death stone carver's doltish lad
And shows him sights that few men ever had?
Oh tell me 'fore in fairness I despair!'

6 - Greek goddess of the moon.

Julianna smiled and touched his tawny cheek.
'If this be dream,' he sighed, 'Dream, dream again
Just throw my brittle bones in brown-crust creek
And leave my spirit here in wild dream glen'
Julianna turned and laughing would not speak

x

Then gliding through that aurelian bright free night
She sang a song of beauty's lasting glance
Of lovers caught in love's sweet-sour trance
And duty's power fading from its might
Hard he chased her through the spirous Yew
Calling 'Galatea! Daphne! Kleio! Thalia! Grace!' [7]
To one so fair of form and soft of face
He pledged undying love and gratitude
Then twisting in his sheets of tattered cloth
Passiano woke and spied a flutt'ring in its pyre
A lone and searching singe-ing summer moth
Caught in life's sweet lovely seeking fire
A searing coat of crimson brightly dothed

xi

'Oh dying moth speak, speak those words of yore
'Fore Daphne's laurel praying heaven speeds
To veil my inner vision's sorest needs
Assure me of sweet beauty's golden ore!'
No voice responded from the fleck of red
No word of surcease sounded from the fire
No angel sought to lift him from that mire
But darkness crept about his lonely bed
He cursed his dream as fruit beyond his reach

---

7 - Galatea, statue of Pygmallion that is brought to life.
Daphne, a river nymph pursued by Apollo, who is turned
into a laurel tree. Kleio, the Muse of music, song and dance.
Thalia, one of the Graces, a group of fertility goddesses.

The flowing robes, the tender laughing glance
The beauteous maid that still refused his speech
The ancient scent of flowering romance
He wondered if he dared to eat that peach

xii

Then through that fateful night he watched the skies
And ere the gloaming dawn had touched the land
He decided with his coarse unruly hand
To fashion firm those sylvan elvan eyes
Quick to the quarry, fast in his resolve
To find a rock the weight of eighty stone
To sculpt his inward vision there alone
And rare eternal beauty there evolve!
What tutelage for this task he had to show
Was chipping off the names of new dead souls
To mark the earth for those who wished to know
Who journeyed hence between those distant poles
Undaunted hard he struck the starting blow

xiii

The marble's flakes fell useless to the floor
The shapeless stone assailed refused to form
That lump of rock left sculptor sore forlorn
As chisel's bite bit closer to the core
Then dark one spirit night, one windswept eve
The hammer mute denounced his lack of skill
The rising moon had just begun to fill
His little shack with moonlight's still belief
There on that soft white light a song was heard
A song of heaven's rapture new endowed
Kalliope then appeared, a snow white bird
Upon an effervescent snow white cloud
She bid him work his work without a word

xiv

With one tremendous blow the stone was split
And as the island-fruit its milk will pour
A marble statue formed of earth-rock's core
Stood flowing fair now free of earthen bit
She seemed to dance though still that lady white
Her arms o'er spread 'neath heaven's boundless grace
That curving form, so soft, that haunting face
Had come at last to him that winter's night
But the surging joy he felt was soon forgot
As cold and still she stood in new morn's hour
He called to her, 'Ah, love' she answered not
Like ice upon a bending meadow flower
He stood before her cursing harsh his lot

xv

Through ceaseless days he watched her image there
And sleepless nights he pledged his love and prayed
For life to come unto the beauteous maid
And morn' to end the darkness of his care
'Oh maid beyond the star-gate unaware
I beg you fix the price that must be paid
To entice you from your proud and moon-swept glade
Oh tell me for in fairness I despair!'
No word, no sign, the figure blind would speak
As Passiano fell below it as in death
In pain untold the boy-man wept alone
His tears raw-streaking on those legs of stone
His eyes grew dark until he sensed a breath
Until he felt a hand upon his cheek

xvi

'Love brings love as love is want to do
And lover's tears are no uncommon sight

Nor that embrace which lovers hold each night
Come, show me that your cries of love are true'
Her voice was fair as there she stood anew
Not stone but maiden-flesh of curving white
With flowing robes, with emerald bodice tight
And elvan eyes of deepest turquoise-blue!
'Rise my heart, no shame in lover's care
And stroll with me beneath the morning star
As Antaeus[8] from the earth my spirit comes
Now walk with me beneath the rising sun'
Softly then she lead him from that place
And gently wiped the sorrow from his face

xvii

They laughed and walked till night had come and then
They left the woods and journeyed to the sea
And there they set their lover's passion free
And laughed and walked till morning came again
Julianna bore him many children there
Green glorious trees and crystal sapphire streams
The lights that haunt a city dweller's dreams
Red-golden clouds and sunlight's yellow hair
Neither food nor drink did Passiano need
Nor company of brutish human-kind
But her sweet form was bread and wine and sleep
And her light laugh was company to keep
Him satiate down the roads of limb and mind
Where men recall that what they are's divine

xviii

Oh the years they passed a blissful path and when
Their nightly walks were spied, their revelry

---

8 - The son of Poseidon and Gaia, Antaeus is
indefatigably strong as long as he remains in
contact with his mother, the earth.

A youthful god and lump of stone were seen
Both visions queer within the sphere of men
Yet those that saw those sights beyond compare
Saw clearly what they had was what it seemed
They knew the tattered filth that belched and reamed
From out their stacks was merely dust filled air
Many a blind and foolish heart spoke not
Yet many more with sight were blessed anew
Passiano felt that spark, that holy fire
Lift him like a leaf, then lift him higher
To see the resurrection of the Yew
And cry the sweetness man had long forgot

xix

Still men like shores the waves of time despoil
Too soon their nightly trysts of love had ceased
Too soon Passiano's youthful face was creased
With lines of care and blemishes of toil
His serpent skin hung loose and pallid wide
His mind was numbed, the pain of life was eased
Julianna with his love had well been pleased
But now she faced the ebbing of his tide
She, immortal, little understood
The gift of fate that men should pass away
Or why they feared to leave the strife of earth
When higher realms awaited their re-birth
She cared for him as long as he would stay
Then kissed his lips when he had passed away

xx

Slowly the understanding dawned in her
That men were caught within their weakness' arms
And dealt themselves and sundry general harms
And clung to hopes and cherished joys that were

And so she laid him down into the earth
The him that had two legs, two eyes and arms
The him that heeded mortal-made alarms
She buried him and sang to him a dirge
Then walking through those woods they'd known in spring
She shed one tear and called Kalliope's name
She begged the burden from her be withdrawn
She begged to be releasèd with the dawn
She sang a song of longing, song of pain
Still knowing that her burden must remain

xxi

Atys[9], demon-time, what dice you throw!
The fabric of our world you etch and weave
Then lead us forth where few do still believe
You take our little lives, why? none do know
Still here at last we find our tale's home
Julianna with one tear was human made
No longer free to walk that moon-swept glade
No longer seen a lump of shapeless stone
And as that jewelèd tear the earth did drink
Those hapless creatures man did new awake
And wondered of the paths they long had roamed
And as this verse, at last they sought their home
Inspired by the beauty man could make
Julianna lingers on and lingers still, I think

And how long will she linger here? None may know
Oh blow wanton winds, winds of wonder blow!

---

9 - Mythological figure representing the twofold
character of nature, the male and female.

The Graal Gate [10]

(with nods to G. Ch. & E. S.)

In th'olde dayes of Arthour te King   *Arthur*
when buds of Avril died i'spring   *April*
an' trials an' terrors happening
to knickt and serf and maiden fair   *knight*
within the darkness pond'ring thir

Te solempne quest knickts failed save one
O! they laye dead beneath the sonne   *sun*
in greene mede and bryre or on hye towre
in bowres where crystal rivers run

The Graal King laughed to see the sport
of humane deere brought down by darts
in day when the land was "fulfild of fairye   *faries*
the elf-queene with hir joly compaignye"
yet 'midst his gate a poet stood
a staff for pen a quilt for hood
unbowed by th'approaching brood

'Gainst tha' comin wood-sturm this Britoun –   *storm*
fed from the cradle changed i' the bed
a changling, yea, of elfin blood
nursed on jolinesse and lust abedde
who chose to be widwe an' wedde   *married*
raised his staff to ward the blows
of elfe warriors, fairye kin and kith
clear seeing their clamour ramping vain
he pledged the' wol nat his honour stain

Yet not for honour nor vaine-say 'lone
he held the gage against the throne   *pledge (of battle)*
of the haughty Graal King wrothèd fild   *angry*
whose gost eyes hurled sparkles fiery red

---

and starèd on all that him beheld
as ashes pale of hew and ded   *hue and dead*

And that Faerie Queene fyne and ydrad   *perfect and dreaded*
who swal with griefe and deadly bale   *evil*
to see wha she taught a heartliss male
b'stride the bridge to the conseil cup
lothly contrarie their sovereinetee wille
wikked her heart with mordre fillèd   *murder*

Doom she shriked to elfe and fairye
loose the dogs of hell and warye
bloosom pixa wolf and satyre
clear th'parage and your words dispende
and to this bishrewen bring 'n ende   *wicked person*
peas–pod harpin flame and brenne
breem this manling to his enne   *clean (debris)*

Ne digne the poet fought in vaine
'gainst magik sublte toothe en straunge
tha' roste and seethe, broile an' frye
mortreux him to the marybones   *stew his marrow bones*
couthe free his sanguin pers and reed s   *spill his blood*
and thresshe his flesh to the sacred mede   *thresh / meadow*

'N when there then the battle donne
the King and Queen in gloria comme
the' held thir dogs wit a fire boone
an' comded that the' be told anoone
the final wirds of the witless prey
an' hir is whot tho elfe d' say

He fought us will tha' jolly avaunter –   *boaster*
pruddeste 'til he be ylimed   *proud until caught (like a bird)*
wi lash and blade an tooth ne sharpen
draggèd to his nees entwined
I fight to hold this door hird to

for you he sayn and you and you
That ye may drinken then tha cup
an' i' tha drinken surcease find
from sorrows balefull misdeeming chaine
drinke m' kinfolke will ye maine?

An' Lady rune-wrappèd neath hi breast
win we had scatter'd sinew widen
as ye commanded us an' chiden
thi wa found, the bright sprite bowed
an from a sheepskin thir unwrappèd
an elfin hearte blud reed and beating   *blood red*
from the foe ripped har anon
thi the battle spoils wonne

The tall Lady gaspa seen the hearte
the final wirds, thou churlish sprite
speak lest I cast you to the ashe
madame hi la breat was-to-thee
tell th'ydrad Faerie Queen, said he
tha I am she and she is me
tha we are we tha we are we
spok'n he his lips no more
'n thi is how we closèd thy door

The Graal King-wi-Queen the' tooken up
the heart to cooke an' to suppe
but from fairye elfe and hounde hell
all long toothe to the shiten pup   *old and young*
the' held the meel an' wi held the cuppe
tha may ya makke lifen worth liven
thi the 'ward tha the' were given

Requiem Mass

I've gone to sleep and – seen the burning – of the
night sky – deep with yearning – deep with dreaming
– past the star fields – where a bright light – yields a
rare field

Gone_to_sleep_and_seen_the_burning_of_the
_night_sky_deep_with_yearning_deep_with
_dreaming_past_the_star_fields_where_a_
bright_light_yields_a_rare_field

Heaven! and beyond – no – end – less – burn
– ing – fires – to – come

Heaven! and the Light!

Sleep_and_dream_the_light_of_being_in_the
_ether_beyond_seeing_beyond_knowing
_beyond_feeling_in_the_ether's_potent_reeling

Beneficial! Maledictus! Mercy's soft touch! Sin will
pass us! And the holding! Of that rare dream! Dim
with time's mist! And your hair seems!

Fire!

Fire!

On_my_face_your_scent_remaining_through
_the_tears_its_faint_touch_straining

Fire!

Fire!

Now – no – more – to – be

Soft – as sunlight's birth – you're touch was once
   the touch of earth's – sweet – loaming – dawn

Sweet – as hill's of green – you're laughter seemed
– bedewed upon – soft – rolling – heaths

Soft_as_sunlight_new_arising_as_the_tyrant
_envious_evening_from_the_garish_day
_long_spending_took_your_hand_to_end
_the end – ing – of – your – song

Sweet_as_icy_streams_a_leaping_down_the
_summer's_meadows_tending_small_white
_flowers_in_their_bower's_dew_remem
– ber – ing – your – song

Your song

And the earth now – dull and weary – in its coldness
– I am emptied – of life's purpose – and the dark ache
– and the beauty – I must forsake

And_the_earth_now_dull_and_weary_in_its
_coldness_I_am_emptied_of_life's_purpose
_and_the_dark_ache_and_the_beauty
_I_must_forsake

Here! Left behind – to – await – the
– tears – to – come

Emptied! and alone – hope – ing – for
– the – dawn

The_dawn – the_dawn – the – dawn

Hush – now my sweet – to let go here – is a feat
– fit for gods – I'm a man – I will do – as I can
– to come to you – free of grief – free of tears

– free of – hate – if you'll wait – by that shore
– this storm will pass – and what's more
– you will smile – for my fate – small or great
– love's reward – ours to share – ours in hope
– and despair – unnamed – you'll – see – us – home

Us – home

And beyond the – sun's bright shining – and the
moon light's – dim reflecting – of its glory – sears
the darkness – without ending – and its pouring
– milk of kindness – blessèd healing – life returning
– and the feeling – of death freeing – limbs a trembling
– from their bondage – from their ending

Christe forté! In the grave there!

Christe morté! Death enslaved there!

Christe tuum est! Death defeated!

Christe Vincit! Mercy treated!

And_the_ashes_back_to_ashes_and_the_dust
_there_back_to_dust_there

Eléison! Eléison! now – no – more – to – be
– where

I hasten to my death – my death – my death_my
death_my death!
I hurry through my life – my life – my life_my
life_my life!

With you – with her –
With you – with – her –
With – you – with – her –
With – you – with – her –

You – her – you –
Her – you

Her!

You!

Her!

And!

You_you_you_you_you

You – you – you – you

You!!

You!

Lochinvar Returns
(with a nod to S.W.S.)

Lochinvar returns
from the east
to the tattered remains
of a widdin' feast
still faithful in love
and undaunted in war
and unshaken by takin'
this road he abhors

Lochinvar
is heard to say
'O! how I remember
that widdin' day
and that laggard in love
that dastard in fight
who I'll lie in his coffin
clad in white
a laird on a dais
that dastard in war
I'll lie in his coffin
by the shore'

At Clan Netherby gate
broadsword in hand
blind Lochinvar barks
a cold command
'come forth ye traitorous
sowlin' teats
and face the wroth
that I must meet
ye here where once
your honor vain

stood for ought
than greed and pain

'Come forth I say
and meet thy end!
with friend or friendless
for I portend
the end of thy wicked
wanton ways
and the end of thy seed
to the end of days!'

So Lochinvar
is heard to rage
yet none come forth
neither laird nor page
from that crumblin' hall
to take the gage
of that grayin' knight –
to take up his curse
to take up his fight

There young Lochinvar
once boldly strode
to take the fair Ellen
to have and hold
'gainst her father's will
from that churlish laird
so bold and impassioned
his words were heard

Throughout the feast
as gailiard they danced
to the coward bridegroom's
shame and scorn
and clan Netherby's infamy
who stood and fumed

at their far–bride and the knight
who'd wooed in good faith
till her father had packed her
off for fame
and coffers of gold
the more to their shame

But out the hall–door
hand on steed he laid
our hero there tossed
that fairest maid
and rode off t'wor' the fens
'fore Forsters, Fenwicks
and Musgraves
they rode and they ran
there racing and chasing
on Cannobie Lee
but the lost bride of Netherby
ne'er did they see'

For across the wil' waves
that break from the east
those lovers set sail
t'wor' a nether shore
to abandon their homeland
ever–more
and for their love's hope
a home to make

There on a green isle
they made their way
they made their love
they made there play–
fulness and their young
heart's soar
in hopes of joy
forever–more

Or so they thought
it must surely be
for so may the good–
hearted blindly see
their world as if
it were as true
as young lovers
in love's tawny hue

Aye! on that star–green
island round
they had set their feet
to a road upon
which lay those hopes
and dreams a'flower
dauntless in an undying hour

A tower they raised
on a high rocky height
that she may gaze
t'wor' that leeward shore
and that child–home forsaken
ever–more
through those mists that chill
those winds that bite

And bright as the fire
of lover's arms
their guilt was 'suaged
their fears were calmed
they rocked their hearts
in a canopied cradle round–
in' fair and strong and able

Three the sons
she bore him there
and one the daughter

wi' raven hair
yet in his eyes
she grew more fair
with each new joy
the passin' years

Yet back 'mong the clans
a hatred rankled
as talk of his shame
spread wide and long
a brier-vine rank
that his pride abhorred
he beat the bloody drums
of war

Aye! that cuckold laird
his heart did burn
with murderous shame
to do him harm
who took tha' prize
he had na' earned
and showed him false
before the clans

S'in secret sent he
rough-necked spies
to find their place
of bliss and gain
a way to end
his coward's shame
and steal that hope
that he despised

'Ndaunted the years
he sought them far
sendin' minions
yon and near

until at last
a word was heard
of a tower-laird
and lady wise

Upon a rocky
island jut
a lonely tower
raisèd high
a solitary
rare abut
an abutment to
a sky-blue sky

And on that green-
gray rollin' shore
a sham' o'huts
but little more
had grown into
a settlement
of those who shunned
the Queens and Lords

Of those who sought
to live in peace
and joy and love
and restful ease
of those who fled
the hypocrites
the power mad
the tyrannies

And of those blisses
they did horde
sweet-milk, brown-bread
and comity
the sea-wind's spray

the moonlight's pale
their neighbor's generosity

Of all the blessin's
they did horde
deep in their heart's
reciprocity
their lady-fair's
forgivin' ways
and gentle heart
'bove all they praised

Yet of Lochinvar
an unease grew
amid the people's
merriment
his solitary
haunts the due
where he was seen
to there commune
with bird and stream
and wander 'bout
as in some dream

'A fairer face
ya cou' na wish'
the fishwife to
the cobbler sighed
'yet such a sadness
in his eyes
yes such a sadness
in his eyes'

'I heerd he wanders
'neath the stars
when folks in-their-beds
they ought to be'

the grouser nodded
to the smith
'still as for that'
the man decreed
'he's ever been a kind
to me and mine'

'It's said a high
born laird was he'
the seamstress to
the tanner leaned
'who shunned his folk
and privileged life
to take our lady
for his wife –
eeer, as our fisher
marm's prone to say
'tis a sadness keeps
him closed away'

Just so those North Sea
years lagged on
lest on some walk
you'd chance upon
that agin' Scot
and his hidden fear
and felt a cold wind
whistlin' near

'Twas past the time
of tempest–seas
and the gentle turn
of spring's caress
the purple heather's
spongy ease
and the south–wind's
gentle warmin' breath

That–back–late one day
the fish–men rowed
with panicked tales
of boats and oars
beyond the break
the clan–laird's horde
there beat the bloody
drums of war

'To arms!' they called
'To arms!' they went
to gather up
their armament
what little arms
they had to show
they gathered up
to ward the blow

Of seasoned blood–
stained men and bold
cold–slayers of
the weak and old
they'd come for their
master's recompense
to slaughter all
the innocents

On the tower steps
Lady Ellen came
callin' many
there by name
'come bring to me
your young, your frail
pick up some stone
some torch, some nail
to fling–back those
who've come to slay

four hundred hands
they'll meet this day
To the tower I say
when ere you may
four hundred hands
they'll meet this day'

And as those death–
boats keeled the shore
a trumpet from
the tower on high
yes! from that tower
a cry of war
rent the golden–
azure sky

And out road
our Lochinvar
to the test
once last on that steed
that was the best
in all the border–
land near and wide
'ya ha!' he clasp
his reins to ride
and save his (good) sword
he weapons had none
he rode all unarm'd
and he rode all alone

Splash!
leapt those clansmen
their kilts in the spray
as their claymores glowed red
with the end of the day
but 'fore they could reach
to that dry rocky shore

a rider rose up and and
down came his sword
severin' head
and sinew and bone
he dealt them many
a mortal blow and
through their hot ranks
a panic spread
as the sea-tide turned
a bloody red

Down yon and forth
Lochinvar stalked those banks
dealt cold death
amongst those ranks
who'd come from that
cuckold laird to gain
the debt that he'd
prepared to pay
so long ago
and so far away
now Lochinvar faced
its forfeiture day

A'rear the clans
black-boot on a bow
a dark captain rose
to bark commands
upon his head
a death-mask helm
within his hand
a jagged blade

And-with-this
the foe-men
closed around
that horse and rider

set upon them
from that tower
high on the heights
they raised their swords
that lord to smite

Gash! the great-horse
'en keeled to a fall
gutted in a bloody ball
but still Lochinvar
held at bay
a score of swords
within that spray

Slash! drew a claymore
from chin to ear
a bloody line
beneath his beard
another pierced
his shield arm
a third cut clean
aside his palm

And as his guard
glossed slick with blood
and his legs grew weary
in the flood
as his sword tip drooped
his foe pressed on
from either side
there rose alarms

From north o' the tower
the-able-town-folk poured
with blade and spear
upon that horde
and at their front

a young maiden fair
with silver cap
and raven hair

And from the south
her brothers came
callin' out
their father's name
upon proud steeds
with silver manes
with silver gild
upon their reins

Through-the-clan they cut
a bloody swath
to their father's side
a gory path
then from the rocks
they pulled him sound
then swung around
and gave them ground

Who now in riotous
clamor yell
on slippery rocks and
this way fell
and that as the good folk
pressed with glee
to beat them back
into the sea

The dark captain saw
his peril clear
and gathered to him
men and brave
an' 'pon the corpses
he did wade

to solid ground
his purpose grave

To raze that tower
to the ground
with the old the lame
the meek the young
to turn the tide
of battle 'round
and from his master
with renown
to steal one lady
scores he'd slay
and for his master
burn that day

'Go! back t'wor' the shore
again and charge!
I'll bind my wounds
and follow hard'
Lochinvar urged
his sons around
then on one knee
fell to the ground

But the battle-joy
that gave him ease
to see the clansmen's
miseries
was soon forgot
as he raised his gaze
to the dark captain
near the tower's base

'To the tower!' he cried
and gained his feet
staggered forward
feet o'er hands

'To the tower, my sons!'
he did entreat
as a fire–glow lit
those rocky lands

For Lochinvar then
the moment slowed
as–if–the azure hour's
sands were stemmed
he spied his sons
to battle go
heedless there
to comprehend
he spied his daughter
sword in hand
urge the erstwhile
town–folk on
as he staggered up
to the tower's height
dragged his sword
upon the ground

High top that tower
'bove blacken smoke
she shone, his white–lady
with the raisèd arms –
above the clamor
some words she spoke
(he aid–less there
to comprehend)
but hoisted children
down long ropes
their mothers wails
the night b'cried
till the fires 'bout
her legs rose up

an' in a sheet a flame
his lover died

Blooded with hate
Lochinvar's heart flamed
then
with rage his sinew's
strength returned
blooded with hate
his cry did rend
the cracklin' night
as the tower burned
above him –
to its base he sprung
down came his sword
upon the foe
from shoulder to waist
the first he cleft
then sent another's
head to roll

Still hotter than
the furnace' flame
his blade upon
the foe–men blazed
until about him
in a rove
a dozen corpses
twisted laid

'Gainst shadowy rocks
the dark captain cowed
his arms outstretched
aghast he cried:
'It was not by me
your lady died!

it was not by me
your lady died!
I begged her down
the stairs to come
but she refused
the deed is done!'

Then Lochinvar 'round
his shoulders grapp'ed
to lift
that coward captain high
and swing him
screamin'–'round he thrust
him 'midst those flames
that licked the sky

And in horror there
the town–folk spied
him hold that captain
'midst the fire
in horror there
his daughter spied
the flames about
his arms and face
heard pitiable screechin'
pierce the air
as her father c'lapsed
near the tower's base

And he would have died there
'neath those walls
but she braved the
singe–in' flamin' through
and pulled him to
but the husk she bore
was not the father
that she knew

For a fortnight groaned
he as in death
belabored in each
staggered breath
a horror-mask where
those flames had lit
his soul's great pain
'cross his face had writ

Yet his sons and daughter
by him there
nursed him with
a patient care
and that daughter
wi' the raven hair
she rallied the town-folk
from despair

And marshaled there
their energies
to rebuild what
was burned and razed
but the ruin of that
tower's base
she left intact
to her parent's praise
charred-black
its jagged stonework rent
it seemed a fittin' monument

When a fortnight passed
with gasps of woe
Lochinvar awoke
within a throw of horror there –
in his ravaged eyes
a shadow lay
a darkness blottin'
out the day

'O Ellen!' he clasped
his daughter's hand
'I-cou'-na run to you
I cou' but stand
and watch you
strugglin' in that fire
'twas my weakness
built your funeral pyre!'

'Hush, father, dear
your Ellen's here
in all the children
that she saved
look! by your feet
fresh flowers and tithes
honor both your sacrifice'

'M'darlin'! M'dear!
was my awful pride
that burned our lives
away to ash
and caught ya helpless
in its flames
your love is gone
my shame remains!'

'Hush, father, please
your sons now strain
to raise a wall of whitest stone
'pon the watery graves
of our enemy
to honor both your memory'

Then with-a-sigh he
shut his eyes to sleep
those burned-out eyes
ne'er more to weep

For nigh on a year
no-further-word he spoke
but nurtured there
his strength and true
within the people's
lovin' care
where-with his children's
greatness grew

And to that place
in boats they sailed
when word of these deeds
blew through the isles
they came to breathe
free air and 'scape
the hate and war
and wasteful trials

Of the clan lairds
caught in golden chains
their fears and fancies
buffetin'
them here them there
with bootless cries
with senseless hearts
with sightless eyes

And these were welcomed
who would share
that peace in life
without the crown
and that daughter
wi' the raven hair
new christened their isle
'White Lady Down'

'Twen again
was past the time

of tempest-seas
and the blindin' fleece
of winter's ash
where huddled hopes
the ewe-lamb's ease
from the north-wind's
waspish bitin' lash

Alone on the cliffs
in 'at burnt ring o' stone
alone Lochinvar stood
scarred hands on chest
as below the people
merry made
to celebrate
past victory

A year to the day
he spoke again
as a single clover
laid he down
'My heart, I vow
now my bitter fate
to go and wait
'fore that bitter gate
where once I took you
for my own
'spite-these-eyes I'll make
that gate my home

'Until I join you
gladly dead
or that villain
on my sword has bled!
with crippled hands
I clasp my fate
and go now
to that bitter gate!'

Then, bent-Lochinvar
set sail once more
back 'cross the sea
to that lee-ward shore
not knowin' that
the foe he sought
for his bloody deed
an end had bought
at the hands of the clans
for Lady Ellen's sake
they had hanged that coward
from his manor gate

Where–

Lochinvar returns
from the east
to the tattered remains
of a widdin' feast
still faithful in love
and undaunted in war
and unshaken by takin'
this road he abhors

and save his (good) sword
he weapons (has) none
he (leans) all unarm'd
and he (leans) all alone...

Amric Loves the Night

Amric loves the night they say
And nightly from his earthen grave
He rises forth and ventures north
To haunt the sacred river's course

Where oak and elm and rowan twine
'Round deep and darkling knotted pine
The grove they call there 'Lover's End'
There Amric walks the woods again

'Faith – Faith' in a mournful tone
The ancient wraith is heard to moan
Where sage and thyme and clover grows
Where stone–cut Estulwaning flows

'Twas long ago that Amric strolled
Amidst those trees in autumn's cold
A love, his heart to hold that night
Enfold her in the dimming light

The setting sun was bright orange–red
And shimmered on the river's bed
When swift he paced in 'Lover's End'
In a glen where Estulwane still wends

Quick brown–dry snaps brought footsteps fast
His o'er late love had come at last
He stood there to meet her to greet her and say
'You've tarried my lovely 'tis long past the day'

His Faith was fifteen, her witch–wood hair
About her shoulders bounced on air
Running to hug him she clung to him tight
And there they lay in the dim starlight

Amric remembered the days of their youth
The times they had played the hurts he had soothed
Six years her elder he held her to be
The rarest flower the fairest to see

Yes! Amric loved those nights when long
Long he'd hold her till the dawn
Alone, their love or so he thought
But that eve's bliss was dearly bought

For through the trees on that dark night
The autumn east-wind howled with fright
Young Faith was betrayed a smithy's rage
Had wrought for her a jealous cage

Den the blacksmith's 'prentice boy
Had followed her unto their joy
And there he spied his heart's desire
And planned for Faith her funeral pyre

Many's the time within their town
Den watched her walk and followed 'round
The shops in hopes the lust to tell
That close within his coal-heart dwelled

Face of soot and hands of steel
Her soft skin he longed to feel
The unmarred whiteness of her arms
That sun-like likeness of her charms

But her tryst there it scored Den's heart
Behind a bush he squat apart
Chewing the bone the gristle of spite
Vowing with his blade to strike!

Amric stroked Faith's tangled hair
And laughter woke without despair

Within that cold he felt no chill
Within her arms he felt no ill

'Soon' he said 'We shall be wed
When your father's fears are fully fled'
Then raising a blanket up over her head
They rested on their forest bed

The blanket shroud it deadened the sound
Of the approaching closing heinous hound
The blade of desire leapt from its sheath
And red–kissed the sleeping child at peace

Not one sigh or muffled cry
Was heard as Amric's Faith died
But he awakened as from a dream
And in torment grasped the deadly scene

In their struggle the blade fell free
And Amric over his knee bent he
Who slew his Faith to the river's bed
He crushed the creature to its death

Swift within that bobbing wave
Den had found his jagged grave
Down the stream his corse did dance
To please death's wholly wholesome glance

Still beside his black–eyed flower
Amric knelt one final hour
He felt the coldness of his loss
He felt the coming of the frost

With that knife that pruned her life
He sought an answer to his strife
With bright steel–sharp he sliced his arms
And dealt himself sore mortal harms

Soft he laid beside her there
Soft wept into her witch-wood hair
Mingled and joined their blood blood red
Forming their eternal bed...

And now of autumn nights it's told
That man and beast both once thought bold
Are afraid to face in that leafless place
The wraith still searching for his Faith

Yes! Amric loves the night they say
And nightly from his earthen grave
He rises forth and ventures north
To haunt the sacred river's course

WILLIAM DRISCOLL

The Poet of Sen Sel–Amar

All are architects of Fate,
Working in these walls of Time;
Some with massive deeds and great,
Some with ornaments of rhyme.
                    ~Longfellow

'I am the poet of Sen Sel–Amar
hearken me people from near and afar
come to me children of Sen Sel–Amar
and hear what I would say

'I am known as the poet of Sen Sel–Amar
but I come from the kingdom Penelopus–Tar
where poets are persecuted thrown to the hounds
and the woeful's doleful injustice abounds

'Oh my dark kingdom in the dark hills of doubt
where lyric and limerick are strictly cut out
of all would be poets dear Sen Sel–Amar
now hear of the land of my youth

'I was an urchin of ten, a rhyme did I make
and for my small laugh a finger they did take
from my knuckle, to teach me of Penelopus–Tar
the land in the dark hills where no poets are

'You see poets were banned by the queen in a rage
when succeeding in finding her like on a page
of poetry infamous in Penelopus–Tar
a satire posted by Regius Lazar

'Regius was buried in the woods they say
and the lords outlawed poetry that very same day
there I was a lad and rhymes were my joy
so quickly I became a finger–less boy

'As I grew older I kept my mouth shut
for I knew not which digit next would be cut
but I rhymed in my head as I lay in my bed
and the fire in my chest grew robust and red

'When into my manhood they trusted me not
(for my love of the limerick was not forgot)
to damn the source of my creative springs
they put out my eyes with two red hot rings

'Oh my life then was lonely dear Sen Sel–Amar
in the land in the dark hills where no poets are

'I begged for my livelihood and bided my time
while still in my head I continued to rhyme
for my spirit wasn't broken as days went their way
'twas my wit that preserved me despite the decay

'One day, I convinced a young lad to write down my lines
and out of my head I dredged up my rhymes
I bid him then post them in the kingdom's confines
the kingdom of Penelopus–Tar

'Then when I was hunted by guards in the night
far from the dark hills I stumbled in flight
I was led by my lad to the shores of this sea
Sen Sel–Amar where poets are free!

'On that first day I stood here my words turned to song
and you came and you gathered and listened quite long
to all the joy lain lost in my pain
soon Sen Sel–Amar you joined my refrain

'You fed me, embraced me and soothed the scar
of my journey from boyhood in Penelopus–Tar
you called me the poet of Sen Sel–Amar
and long have I lingered among you

'Now as I stand on these shores at the end of my days
dwelling on the passing of countless by–ways
and the poor queen's commands for spite of my verse
that was meant as a kinder reminder of mirth

'Come, grieve with me people from near and afar
for the happiness silenced in Penelopus–Tar…'

Saying this the poet faced straight out to sea
as if on the white waves he could be free
then slumping to sitting with one short breath
the poet set sail for the kingdom of death

There still he cites lines to all who will hear
some laugh at his rhymes and pass in good cheer
but for some he saves the tale of Penelopus–Tar
the land in the dark hills where no poets are

The Golden Bird

The remembrances
of an ancient Puka–pu
native on his death bed
transcribed by the right
honorable Reverend
Mr. Goodmarker
during his travels to
the island of
Milestogoandmore
the year of our Lord 1912

'Oh God
whom in thine infinite
wisdom
has granted me
divine ignorance
fill me
that I may be inspired
to glean clearly
the subject
and interpret diligently
the final words
of Elu 'bright–eye'
late shaman of the
Puka–pu's
though pagan–filled
with lifelong folly
at the last
quite unbeknownst
to himself
a baptized member
of Thy holy order'

~Rev. G.

'Beating, beating, with the rhythm
beating on the jungle island
six of us we were not many
dancing to the drums

dancing there our youthful dances
dancing to the drums

'Past the time when leaves were weaving
sun was shining on the water
sixteen summers then behind us
and the flower's pink fruit held us
and the tribal elders kept us
from the hila shy

'Came the painting of the faces
reds and yellows like the flowers
I the smallest was encouraged
I the youngest taunted also
six of us to take the journey
for the Golden Bird

'Elu, Ia, Kor and Zon
Mana, Numu were the brothers
Numu asked the elders questions
Ia eyed the hila budding
Kor and Zon stood ever eager
as the morning dawned

'Through the jungle's broad–leaf vistas
over blue and running water
we went forth with spirits soaring
open hands and shining faces
when we came upon a mountain
taller than the trees

'Up the narrow mountain path
Mana pushed ahead of Kor
Zon and Ia fell behind him
I and Numu lingered after
then we heard tall Mana's laughter
from the mountain top

"Far' he told us was his vision
'high' he said above all others
Numu tried to push beside him
Mana threw him down the mountain
Kor then asked a turn to view it
Mana shook his head

'We all called for him to share it
'no' he said and called us lizards
only he would have the mountain
only he the sky and water
'go!' he called as we were children
'seek your tarnished bird'

'On that lofty perch we left him
Numu shook his fist in anger
Kor looked up with eyes of longing
I called out for him to come
but on that proud and lonely peak
was room for only one

'Sorrow fell for Mana's absence
fell like night upon our foreheads
Numu shook his head and cursed him
I fell silent like the turtle
hearing then coarse voices singing
singing songs of love

'Through the deep leafed jungle palm trees
in a flat and rocky cliff-face
there a cave mouth dark and open
issued forth those songs of love
shrill and lilting like the ju ju
were those songs of love

'None of us would dare to enter
but crouched quiet as the kona

from that dark and yawning cliff mouth
leapt five maidens brown and naked
firing us with foreign feelings
calling us to dance

'Goddesses they led us forward
feeding us on ripe red makos
there our boyhood loins were lifted
riding swift on love's white waters
there our naked bodies drifted
on those pools of love

'As the hours passed in rapture
numbing us to increased pleasure
weariness came falling downward
darkness claimed us one by one
only Ia there outlived us
on that battlefield

'In some moonless starless blackness
troubled by some dream of dying
I awoke and gasped in horror
'flee!' I shouted to my brothers
as six blotched and bloated demons
fed upon our flesh

'So we fled into the jungle
fled that place of hidden terrors
ran until our hearts were bursting
huddled there beneath some bushes
in the morning shocked we noticed
Ia had remained

'Soft we snuck back to that clearing
'neath that jagged cliff of longing
Ia's body to recover
our fair Ia like a brother

but our search found only voices
singing songs of love

'With those maidens brown and ripened
there danced Ia golden shining
calling us to join their pleasure
mining there love's deepest treasure
we all called for him to flee there
Ia shook his head

'Again we called for him to leave them
'no' he said and called us women
he would have his heart's desire
he would suck the fruits of passion
'go!' he sneered as we were children
'seek your tarnished bird'

'In that clearing then we left him
Numu shook his fist in anger
Kor looked back with eyes of longing
I called out for him to come
but under that lusty jagged cliff
Ia would remain

'Sorrow fell for Ia's absence
fell like night upon our foreheads
Numu shook his head and cursed him
I looked downward like the sea-bird
spying then a shining valley
opening below

'Through that valley ran a river
sparkling water filled with treasure
we ran down and sifted through it
pebbles gained we fair to gaze on
grew there piles rich before us
as we labored on

'Some gained gold and some fair silver
others blue and crystal pebbles
Kor was ever over shoulder
counting all the shiny treasure
then division he put forward
for the shiny spoils

'Fair dividing of the pebbles
seemed a wise and prudent high road
so that night we had a choosing
each took turns till all was taken
and when all was said and done
only Kor complained

'He claimed Numu got the greatest
Zon the gold and I the silver
we all laughed hard at his statements
he then sulked and would not join us
looking at the piles we wondered
they were all the same

'Late that night as we all slumbered
I awoke to sounds and movement
Kor was taking up our treasure
with his own he piled together
I stood up and asked him why but
he would not explain

'Zon and Numu then awakened
I stopped Numu who would harm him
Zon looked on with puzzled visage
we all asked him why he did it
Kor looked up with eyes of hatred
this is what he said

'Zon he stated was the smartest
Numu strongest, I the fastest

only he had been forgotten
by the Maker been forsaken
and for this he claimed the riches
from the river's bed

'We then begged for his repentance
'no' he said and called us serpents
he deserved the river's treasure
only he the gold and silver
'go!' he spat as we were children
'seek your tarnished bird'

'By that river bed we left him
Numu shook his fist in anger
none looked back with eyes of longing
I shed tears for our lost friend
yet with that shiny glittering hoard
Kor was quite content

'Sorrow fell for Kor's betrayal
fell like night upon our foreheads
Numu shook his head and cursed him
I inhaled like the teel
smelling then the scent of feast-meat
strong upon the wind

'In a rounded copse of palm trees
in the center of a clearing
stood a breadfruit wide and hoary
in its roots an ancient doorway
splitting crack stood gaping open
and from this they came

'Little laughing Pika people
spreading there an ample table
roasted meats and flowing tree fruits
silver fishes from the ocean

all the dishes one could wish for
for a mighty feast

"La la laika' sang the Pikas
Pikas magic pixie people
from their tree-door they came forward
bringing more and more to feast on
laughing then they urged us towards them
calling us to join

'Zon went forward striding fearless
I and Numu close behind him
and the Pikas gathered 'round us
calling each of us by name
sitting us before the feasting
bidding us to start

'There on chairs of palms and flowers
on we feasted through the evening
drinking multi-colored liquors
burning scented leaves and peelings
till our heads were all but reeling
and our bellies round

'Followed countless moons of glutting
stuffings to the point of bursting
laughter filled with colored liquors
and the scent of numbing plants
Li! streaking 'cross my inner mind's eye
flew the Golden Bird

"Come!' I called to Zon and Numu
'there beyond the forest Haru
golden feathers, soaring spirit
flies the Golden Bird
we must leave the ease of feasting
and continue on!'

'Numu gained his feet and followed
Zon said 'no' and called us dreamers
he would have the joy of plenty
he the magic Pika liquors
'go!' he said as we were foolish
'seek your tarnished bird'

'With the Pika's laughs we left him
Numu shook his fist in anger
I felt pity for our brother
'midst those liquor–plants
still with fish and juicy feast meats
Zon was quite content

'Sorrow fell for Zon's withdrawal
fell like night upon our journey
Numu shook his head and cursed him
I peered forward like the boar
seeking there a path to take us
through the forest dense

'On we labored, I and Numu
through the Haru, dead man's forest
long forbidden to our people
maze and tangled thick root jungle
soon we lost our feasting's roundness
in the Haru there

'On we labored without ending
Numu growled and cursed my choosing
I said 'we must keep on going'
struggling through the heat
branches tearing skin red open
chi-chi's in our ears

'Then one night of increased labor
Numu maddened if with fever

blaming me for all our hardships
in the Haru's tangle there
picking up a branch he rushed me
filling me with fear

"I will kill!' you he went crashing
through the forest's branches buzzing
'stop' I pleaded him while running
'brother are you mad?'
'I will kill you!' he repeated
reveling in his rage

'In that forest then I fled him
thrashing all within his arm's reach
calling back for his lost senses
'Ahhhh!' was his reply
'I will kill you little traitor!'
were his final words

'In that fiery mood I fled him
none remained to curse with anger
nor look back with eyes of longing
calling him to come
yet in that wild and angry wood
Numu found his home

'Sorrow fell for Numu's madness
fell like weight upon my shoulders
none were there to look in horror
I hid close and wept till dawn
for in that large and mystic forest
I was left alone

'All the companions of my questing
Mana tall and Numu strong
Zon the wise and Kor the crafty
and fair Ia bright to gaze on

all were lost and yet I knew
that I must journey on

'Days met days of lonely searching
through the forest's mazes maddening
on the brink of death's dark doorway
stumbled I upon a pathway
'round it wove in sun-way circles
till it found its end

'There a rock-mound round and ancient
tall and egg shaped facing eastward
near its grassy door a circle
on its stony face was carved
sun-ways also curling inward
to a central point

'Stilling then my breath I entered
crawling through the earthen doorway
crouching there in coolest blackness
tunnel slanting ever downward
halted breath and heart beat pounding
were the only sounds

'On I went and always downward
till I lost all sense of sunlight
till my world had been forgotten
and myself I had forsaken
darkness and the breath of life
were my companions then

'Low I crept on on my elbows
fighting fears that came to stop me
deep I was with no returning
and before me little knowing
but I forced my bone and sinew
to continue down

'Suddenly the path beneath me
quick gave way and sent me tumbling
down a cleft deep filled with darkness
grasping there for any hand hold
falling fast unto the center
of that chasm there

'As I fell each heart beat fearing
that the crush of bottom breaking
up would swell and crack me open
curling close I closed my eyes
clenching then my muscles tightly
gasping there for air

'Suddenly there came an impact
not sharp stone but water fluid
roiled I plunged into the depths there
flailing arms and legs to right me
surging water cold around me
spinning me with force

'Dreams I had there in that current
waking dreams of hidden import
through the night sky I went soaring
stars and light–beings flying by me
brilliant faces, standing totems
watching as I passed

'And there stood Mana dark to gaze on
and bright Ia's dying body
Zon grown fat and Kor grown wicked
Numu raging through the heavens
and beyond them burning brightness
cold and white it lay

'White as fruit milk Kala-laka
moon and heaven's shinning holder

terror held me as I entered
and my waking eyes were stung
for in that moment of revealing
I beheld the sun

'From a high and rocky cliff face
out I rushed with water falling
soaring day-ward like the sea-bird
spirit still in Kala-laka
as I found the current's ending
I recalled no more

'There before that fall to darkness
in the corner of my day-eyes
I beneath me saw an inlet
lined with trees and bright birds singing
bluest water reaching upward
then I knew no more

'Just how long I lay in darkness
I know not nor none can tell me
but I wakened on a root-bank
legs still bobbing in the water
there my new-born lungs took inward
my first breath of life

'And there beside me stood a vision
lithe and lilting light robed maiden
beauty as the seas that whisper
all the hopes that men hold inward
stooping then she stroked my head
laughing as she soothed

'There she stood tall Heena-ma-ha
lithe and laughing water woman
from the sea of long remembering
from the dreams of youthful dreaming

in her lap I laid my head
and cried there tears of joy

"Hush' she smiled bright Heena-ma-ha
'now's the time for song and laughter
come and taste the fruits of being
and life's waters cold and shining'
by the hand she led me round
her hidden inlet home

'Sacred inlet Haru-tala
mountain water's secret basin
wonders saw I in the trees there
birds of multi-colored plumage
streams of blue-white leaping fountains
singing in their beds

'Yet 'midst the marvels there abounding
chanting birds as tame as children
streams that sang the song of living
and that mighty water fall
radiant she outshone them all
laughing as she danced

'Yes! in my heart that laughter lingers
and the lessons there unspoken
love for all within the Ra sphere
in my soul was born at last
even for the meanest creatures
crawling on the ground

'And the rocks and trees and waters
came alive with living presence
days passed swiftly in my joy there
joy beyond the words of saying
for my brothers lost in questing
understanding came

'And my love for Heena-ma-ha
love beyond the words of saying
purest love grew ever greenward
like the jungle leaves in springtime
I resigned to live my life there
in that place of joy

'Still as the seventh moon was setting
since my rebirth in those waters
Heena-ma-ha sat beside me
taking soft my hand in her hand
searching in my eyes (adoring)
this is what she said

"Soon our time of joy is ending
and comes swift the time of parting
you must pledge to do my bidding
bright man water-born'
'anything!' I said with feeling
but my heart grew cold

'Taking me unto the clearing
by the water's moon-blue inlet
'short' she said 'your time of sorrow
if you plant me here
and tend this spot with deepest reverence
for my memory'

"Long that time may be in coming'
I spoke boldly and she smiled
'dance with me' she said quite softly
and we danced a dance of life
in that clearing sacred clearing
and my joy returned

'In the morning I awakened
from a fitful night of sleeping

and beside me Heena–ma–ha
cold and dead she lay
moonlight now her sun full setting
and she danced no more

'Bowed with grief, her words recalling
I buried her within that clearing
jungle flowers I spread round her
watering her mound with tears
with no food nor drink nor sleep there
I began my watch

'Guarding there her hallowed grave sight
I made peace to lie beside her
and no bird nor sparkling water
could break my resolve
'Heena–ma–ha I will join you!'
I proclaimed aloud

'Yet as the second day was ending
from the jungle mists surrounding
a voice her voice whispered softly
'live!' was all it said
and I knew my grief was vainness
though my heart protest

'And as that night grew chill and misty
spreading then my arms towards heaven
'Maker' said I 'of the world
I am in your hands
all I do or fail is yours now
help me understand'

'Then as the morning birds woke singing
sun was rising on the water
by my side a burst of sunlight
blinding white light all around me

and the ground began to tremble
and the birds grew still

'Yes! on that third morn from the grave–sight
earth and flowers splitting open
grew a slender golden sapling
fast it grew and ever skyward
years of growth in minutes passing
branches spreading wide

'Fanning leaves that glinted golden
golden fruit too bright for tasting
as the eerie light was fading
flowering full grown
if a hundred years were passing
in those moments there

'Stunned I sat there in that quiet
birds and streams their voices silent
then it rose so slow and softly
from a golden bough above me
music of the gods it lilted
through my mortal soul

'Music as the wind that whispers
o'er the calm sea's hidden splendor
or the sunlight green diffusing
through the forest's flowers and branches
soft it spread and ever lighter
till my being was filled

'Rising to my feet with lightness
lightness as the wings of heaven
in that tree I spied a brightness
small and glowing head held skyward
Li! in that moment I beheld
the little Golden Bird

'Then my body filled with feeling
till my head was all but spinning
to my knees I fell in rapture
there beside that glowing tree
and for a moment I was not –
beneath the Golden Bird

'Still its song grew ever louder
ever sweeter to the hearing
simple beauty joyous tones
spreading through the trees
upward drifting through the heavens
ultimately free

'What a moment for recalling
all my life that song of freedom
truth and rapture not repeated
not repeated and not needed
for my heart that song remembers
and my soul was filled

'Forcing squinting eyes to gaze up
at that brilliance there revealing
from the branch I spied a feather
falling towards my hand
clutching upwards things grew hazy
and I knew no more

'Dreams I had there in that reeling
waking dreams of hidden import
there I was in Kala–laka
moon and heaven's shinning holder
there I reached my hand outstretched
to touch the face of being

'Just how long I lay in darkness
I know not nor none can tell me

but I wakened on the seashore
legs still bobbing in the waves there
in my hand a golden feather
clutching to my breast

'Voices cried then from their kanus
village voices of my people
taking me they paddled homeward
as the dawn grew ever brighter
gazing at my golden feather
they pointed as they rowed

'At the bank our shaman met me
greeting me with increased gladness
in his hut I told my story
and he smiled to hear me tell it
something from his sash he showed me
and I smiled as well

'In his hoary hand quite ancient
shinning brightly of its own light
was a feather like my feather
golden as the sun in summer
in the death-shrine of his fathers
it would rest one day

'And I told him 'fore my passing
mine will rest in likewise keeping
in the death-shrine of my fathers'
and he smiled again
showing me his sash's secret
I kept my feather hid

'And that night there was a feasting
and the people called me blessèd
and the drums beat loud as thunder
and the chanting even louder

all that night our village praised
the blessing I had brought

'But now my soul it walked in two worlds
at the feast and blessed inlet
sacred inlet Haru-tala
Heena-ma-ha dancing by me
Golden Bird its spirit singing
ever after was it so

'Still the years they passed as always
and the seasons rolled their rhythms
in my village I was welcome
and my place secure
'bright-eye' lover true of all things
was my name to them

'And my brothers had their places
Mana was a chief of elders
Ia hila lover peerless
Kor a trader rich in business
Zon a host and Numu fighter
all with more renown

'And I loved them though they spurned me
and they brought the men to envy
but the children flocked around me
and the wise to hear my story
with my place and golden feather
I was quite content...'

Soon after
Elu 'bright-eye'
late shaman
of the Puka-pu's
closed his eyes
and spoke no more

'Heena–ma–ha,
bird of gold!'
were his final words

~Rev. G.

www.ingramcontent.com/pod-product-compliance
Lightning Source LLC
Chambersburg PA
CBHW060709030426
42337CB00017B/2814

* 9 7 8 0 6 9 2 3 3 5 2 9 1 *